LAYERS OF LEARNING

YEAR ONE • UNIT NINE

PERSIANS
ARCTIC
WAVES
MELODY

HooDoo Publishing
United States of America
©2014 Layers of Learning
Copies of maps or activities may be made for a particular family or classroom.
ISBN 978-1494944384

Units At A Glance: Topics For All Four Years of the Layers of Learning Program

1	History	Geography	Science	The Arts
1	Mesopotamia	Maps	Planets	Cave Paintings
2	Egypt	Map Keys	Stars	Egyptian Art
3	Europe	Global Grids	Earth & Moon	Crafts
4	Ancient Greece	Wonders	Satellites	Greek Art
5	Babylon	Mapping People	Humans in Space	Poetry
6	The Levant	Physical Earth	Laws of Motion	List Poems
7	Phoenicians	Oceans	Motion	Moral Stories
8	Assyrians	Deserts	Fluids	Rhythm
9	Persians	Arctic	Waves	Melody
10	Ancient China	Forests	Machines	Chinese Art
11	Early Japan	Mountains	States of Matter	Line & Shape
12	Arabia	Rivers & Lakes	Atoms	Color & Value
13	Ancient India	Grasslands	Elements	Texture & Form
14	Ancient Africa	Africa	Bonding	African Tales
15	First North Americans	North America	Salts	Creative Kids
16	Ancient South America	South America	Plants	South American Art
17	Celts	Europe	Flowering Plants	Jewelry
18	Roman Republic	Asia	Trees	Roman Art
19	Christianity	Australia & Oceania	Simple Plants	Instruments
20	Roman Empire	You Explore	Fungi	Composing Music

2	History	Geography	Science	The Arts
1	Byzantines	Turkey	Climate & Seasons	Byzantine Art
2	Barbarians	Ireland	Forecasting	Illumination
3	Islam	Arabian Peninsula	Clouds & Precipitation	Creative Kids
4	Vikings	Norway	Special Effects	Viking Art
5	Anglo Saxons	Britain	Wild Weather	King Arthur Tales
6	Charlemagne	France	Cells and DNA	Carolingian Art
7	Normans	Nigeria	Skeletons	Canterbury Tales
8	Feudal System	Germany	Muscles, Skin, & Cardiopulmonary	Gothic Art
9	Crusades	Balkans	Digestive & Senses	Religious Art
10	Burgundy, Venice, Spain	Switzerland	Nerves	Oil Paints
11	Wars of the Roses	Russia	Health	Minstrels & Plays
12	Eastern Europe	Hungary	Metals	Printmaking
13	African Kingdoms	Mali	Carbon Chem	Textiles
14	Asian Kingdoms	Southeast Asia	Non-metals	Vivid Language
15	Mongols	Caucuses	Gasses & Kinetic Theory	Fun With Poetry
16	Medieval China & Japan	China	Electricity	Asian Arts
17	Pacific Peoples	Micronesia	Circuits	Arts of the Islands
18	American Peoples	Canada	Technology	Indian Legends
19	The Renaissance	Italy	Magnetism	Renaissance Art I
20	Explorers	Caribbean Sea	Motors	Renaissance Art II

3	History	Geography	Science	The Arts
1	Age of Exploration	Argentina and Chile	Classification & Insects	Fairy Tales
2	The Ottoman Empire	Egypt and Libya	Reptiles & Amphibians	Poetry
3	Mogul Empire	Pakistan & Afghanistan	Fish	Mogul Arts
4	Reformation	Angola & Zambia	Birds	Reformation Art
5	Renaissance England	Tanzania & Kenya	Mammals & Primates	Shakespeare
6	Thirty Years War	Spain	Sound	Baroque Music
7	The Dutch	Netherlands	Light & Optics	Baroque Art I
8	France	Indonesia	Bending Light	Baroque Art II
9	The Enlightenment	Korean Pen.	Color	Art Journaling
10	Russia & Prussia	Central Asia	History of Science	Watercolors
11	Conquistadors	Baltic States	Igneous Rocks	Creative Kids
12	Settlers	Peru & Bolivia	Sedimentary Rocks	Native American Art
13	13 Colonies	Central America	Metamorphic Rocks	Settler Sayings
14	Slave Trade	Brazil	Gems & Minerals	Colonial Art
15	The South Pacific	Australasia	Fossils	Principles of Art
16	The British in India	India	Chemical Reactions	Classical Music
17	Boston Tea Party	Japan	Reversible Reactions	Folk Music
18	Founding Fathers	Iran	Compounds & Solutions	Rococo
19	Declaring Independence	Samoa and Tonga	Oxidation & Reduction	Creative Crafts I
20	The American Revolution	South Africa	Acids & Bases	Creative Crafts II

4	History	Geography	Science	The Arts
1	American Government	USA	Heat & Temperature	Patriotic Music
2	Expanding Nation	Pacific States	Motors & Engines	Tall Tales
3	Industrial Revolution	U.S. Landscapes	Energy	Romantic Art I
4	Revolutions	Mountain West States	Energy Sources	Romantic Art II
5	Africa	U.S. Political Maps	Energy Conversion	Impressionism I
6	The West	Southwest States	Earth Structure	Impressionism II
7	Civil War	National Parks	Plate Tectonics	Post-Impressionism
8	World War I	Plains States	Earthquakes	Expressionism
9	Totalitarianism	U.S. Economics	Volcanoes	Abstract Art
10	Great Depression	Heartland States	Mountain Building	Kinds of Art
11	World War II	Symbols and Landmarks	Chemistry of Air & Water	War Art
12	Modern East Asia	The South States	Food Chemistry	Modern Art
13	India's Independence	People of America	Industry	Pop Art
14	Israel	Appalachian States	Chemistry of Farming	Modern Music
15	Cold War	U.S. Territories	Chemistry of Medicine	Free Verse
16	Vietnam War	Atlantic States	Food Chains	Photography
17	Latin America	New England States	Animal Groups	Latin American Art
18	Civil Rights	Home State Study	Instincts	Theater & Film
19	Technology	Home State Study II	Habitats	Architecture
20	Terrorism	America in Review	Conservation	Creative Kids

Unit 1-9

Printable Pack

This unit includes printables at the end. To make life easier for you we also created digital printable packs for each unit. To retrieve your printable pack for Unit 1-9, please visit

www.layers-of-learning.com/digital-printable-packs/

Put the printable pack in your shopping cart and use this coupon code:

0107UNIT1-9

Your printable pack will be free.

LAYERS OF LEARNING INTRODUCTION

This is part of a series of units in the Layers of Learning homeschool curriculum, including the subjects of history, geography, science, and the arts. Children from 1st through 12th can participate in the same curriculum at the same time -family school style.

The units are intended to be used in order as the basis of a complete curriculum (once you add in a systematic math, reading, and writing program). You begin with Year 1 Unit 1 no matter what ages your children are. Spend about 2 weeks on each unit. You pick and choose the activities within the unit that appeal to you and read the books from the book list that are available to you or find others on the same topic from your library. We highly recommend that you use the timeline in every history section as the backbone. Then flesh out your learning with reading and activities that highlight the topics you think are the most important.

Alternatively, you can use the units as activity ideas to supplement another curriculum in any order you wish. You can still use them with all ages of children at the same time.

When you've finished with Year One, move on to Year Two, Year Three, and Year Four. Then begin again with Year One and work your way through the years again. Now your children will be older, reading more involved books, and writing more in depth. When you have completed the sequence for the second time, you start again on it for the third and final time. If your student began with Layers of Learning in 1st grade and stayed with it all the way through she would go through the four year rotation three times, firmly cementing the information in her mind in ever increasing depth. At each level you should expect increasing amounts of outside reading and writing. High schoolers in particular should be reading extensively, and if possible, participating in discussion groups.

☺ ☻ ☻ These icons will guide you in spotting activities and books that are appropriate for the age of child you are working with. But if you think an activity is too juvenile or too difficult for your kids, adjust accordingly. The icons are not there as rules, just guides.

☺ GRADES 1-4

☻ GRADES 5-8

☻ GRADES 9-12

Within each unit we share:
- EXPLORATIONS, activities relating to the topic;
- EXPERIMENTS, usually associated with science topics;
- EXPEDITIONS, field trips;
- EXPLANATIONS, teacher helps or educational philosophies.

In the sidebars we also include Additional Layers, Famous Folks, Fabulous Facts, On the Web, and other extra related topics that can take you off on tangents, exploring the world and your interests with a bit more freedom. The curriculum will always be there to pull you back on track when you're ready.

You can learn more about how to use this curriculum at www.layers-of-learning.com/layers-of-learning-program/

UNIT NINE

PERSIANS – ARCTIC – WAVES – MELODY

Most books, like their authors, are born to die; of only a few books can it be said that death hath no dominion over them; they live, and their influence lives forever.

-J. Swartz

LIBRARY LIST:

HISTORY

Search for: Persia, Persians, Ancient Iran, Cyrus, Darius, Zoroastrianism

☺ ☻ ☻ The Shahnameh: The Persian Book of Kings by Abolqasem Ferdowsi, Dick Davis trans. Written in the tenth century, this book tells the stories of the ancient Persian kings in epic form. Iranian children grow up hearing these tales. Read aloud in bits for younger kids.

☺ Amoo Norooz and Other Persian Folk Stories by Ahmad Jabari.

☺ ☻ The Red Lion, A Tale of Ancient Persia by Diane Wolkstein. The story of a prince who must face his fears and kill the red lion before he can be crowned king. Not only is this set in the historical time and place of this unit, it is also a great story about facing your fears and having courage.

☻ Ancient Iran by Massoume Price. Colorful basic history of Iran's earliest people.

☻ Arash the Archer: A Story from Ancient Persia by Shahriar Bourbour. This story is about a 12-year-old boy who is a great archer trying to solve a riddle. It includes a lot of figures from Persian mythology and provides a basic introduction to some Zoroastrian philosophy.

☻ The Persian Expedition by Xenophon, Rex Warner trans. An eyewitness account by a Greek who entered Persia on an ill-fated military expedition. Easy to read if you choose the right translation. Read the comments from other readers on various translations to find the one that fits you.

☻ Persian Fire: The First World Empire and the Battle For the West by Tim Holland. A history of the Greek and Persian wars told from the points of view of both sides. Conversational and fun in tone.

☻ The Persians: Ancient, Medieval and Modern Iran by Homa Katouzian. Written by an Iranian, this gives a broad overview of the history of this influential part of the world.

☻ The Persians by Maria Brosius. Covers 1000 years of pre-Islamic Persian history.

☻ I, Demokedes by CJ Wright. Fictionalized story of a real Greek physician who lived during the pivotal time around 500 B.C. While told form the point of view of the Greeks, the story concerns the whole world at that time, including Persia.

GEOGRAPHY	Search for: Arctic, Antarctica, polar regions, polar explorers, tundra ☺ <u>Polar Opposites</u> by Erik Brooks. A polar bear and a penguin are best friends who introduce you to opposites including north/south, up/down, big/small, sweet/sour, and so on. ☺ <u>Draw, Write, Now, Book 4</u> by Marie Hablitzel and Kim Stitzer. Drawing instruction and copy work on a polar theme. ☺ <u>Who Lives Here? Polar Animals</u> by Deborah Hodge. Covers both Arctic and Antarctic animals. ☺ ☻ <u>Polar Exploration: The Heroic Exploits of the World's Greatest Polar Explorers</u> by Beau Riffenburgh and the Royal Geographical Society. ☺ ☻ <u>We Were There on the Nautilus</u> by Robert N. Webb. A fascinating story about a submarine crew attempting to secretly arrive at the North Pole and make the first transpolar trip from the Pacific to the Atlantic. ☻ <u>Science on Ice: Four Polar Expeditions</u> by Chris Linder. Takes the reader through what it's actually like to be a modern polar scientist. Amazing photos.
SCIENCE	Search for: waves, sound, vibrations, light ☺ <u>Day Light, Night Light</u> by Franklyn Branley. Explains properties of light for the very young. ☺ <u>Sounds All Around</u> by Wendy Pfeffer. Clear explanation of the scientific principles behind sound. ☺ <u>Oscar and the Bat: A Book About Sound</u> by Geoff Waring. The science of sound in non-technical language. ☺ <u>The Magic School Bus in the Haunted Museum: A Book About Sound</u> by Linda Beech. ☻ <u>The Science of Sound and Music</u> by Shar Levine. Equal parts science and music, this book is full of hands-on activities for the curious student.
THE ARTS	Search for: melody, children's music; Pick up several children's music CD's with familiar melodies to listen to, sing, and enjoy during this unit. ☺ ☻ <u>M is For Melody</u> by Kathy-jo Wargin. Covers definitions of music styles, terms, instruments and composers. ☺ ☻ ☻ <u>First Steps in Music Theory</u> by Eric Taylor. Graded for 1st through 5th, but certainly useable starting at any age this is a book for the teacher to help kids learn music theory starting at the beginning. Learn it together. ☺ ☻ ☻ <u>The Melody Book: 300 Selections . . .</u> by Patricia Hackett. A collection of songs including children's favorites, folk songs, ethnic, sacred, holiday and more.

HISTORY: PERSIANS

Fabulous Fact

Achaemenid Empire is another name given to the Persian Empire. You may see this word used in some of the reading you do. It's exactly the same people. They called themselves the Parsa. "Persian" comes from the Greeks.

Stuff the Persians Did

Government road and postal systems began with the Persians. They also were the first to establish an official language. They began bureaucracy to control and regulate the empire along with a centralized standing army and civil service.

One other oddity: they released and freed the slaves from the lands they conquered.

Standard of Cyrus the Great

The Persians were the next great empire to rise in Mesopotamia after the Assyrians and Babylonians, but the Persian Empire stretched even further. The great kings of Persia wanted money. They would conquer a people or a city and then exact tribute or taxes. Usually a local would be set up by the Persian king as a ruler over the city and the people could keep their own customs and their own traditions as long as they paid the tribute. The system worked well for Persia since the kings became fabulously wealthy and the people were not so terribly oppressed that they revolted often. The Persians were finally defeated by a people they had tried unsuccessfully to conquer – the Greeks.

☺ ☺ ☻ **EXPLORATION: Persian Empire Map**

Use the Persian Empire map found at the end of this unit. Color the greatest extent of the Persian Empire. Include the road system that connected the empire. The map shows some of the major cities and the various nations that made up the Persian Empire, including Bactria, Israel, Egypt, Elam, Media, Cilicia, Cappadocia, Lydia, Armenia, and Persia itself.

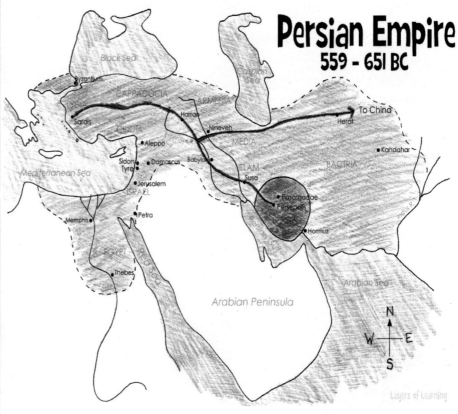

☺ ☺ ☺ EXPLORATION: Make a Persian Timeline

This timeline begins as far back as we have dates and ends at the time of the first Islamic caliphate. Countries in this part of the world are often divided into Pre-Islamic and Islamic time periods. There is a set of printable timeline squares at the end of this unit.

- 1300 BC Medes in the north and Persians in the south settle into cities
- 728-330BC Dynasty of the Medes
- 700-600 BC The kingdom of Edia and the kingdom of Persia are set up
- 559-530 BC Cyrus II (the great) is king of Persia
- 550 BC Cyrus defeats the Medes
- 522-486 BC Darius I is king of Persia and the empire reaches its greatest extent
- 486-465 BC Greeks and Persians go to war
- 486-465 BC Xerxes I, son of Darius, is king of Persia
- 331-330 BC Persia is conquered by Alexander the Great
- 330-312 BC Hellenistic Dynasty
- 312-238 BC Seleucid Dynasty
- 238 BC- 224 AD Parthian Dynasty
- 123 BC – 87 BC Mithradates II (the Great) rules
- 224 – 651 AD Sassanian Dynasty

☺ ☺ ☺ EXPLORATION: Zoroastrianism

Zoroastrianism is the ancient religion of Persia. Long before Muhammad, there was Zarathustra. He was a prophet who rejected the polytheism of his time. He believed in one supreme creator God who could do no evil. Zoroastrian priests are called magi. Their beliefs are surprisingly close to Christian beliefs. Zoroastrianism is practiced by people all over the world still today. Learn more about Zoroastrianism at www.zoroastrianism.com .

☺ ☺ ☺ EXPLANATION: Time Capsule

A great cylinder seal was found by archaeologists at the base of the temple wall in Babylon. It was placed there by command of Cyrus the Great as a time capsule for the future. All over the cylinder is cuneiform writing. It tells the story of the last wicked king of Babylon, Nabonidus, who was overthrown through the will

Photograph by Mike Peel
(www.mikepeel.net)

Additional Layer

Royal families who rule in inherited succession are called a dynasty. It can get murky regarding exactly who is next in line for the throne though. When a dynasty changes from one family to another, there is almost always a great deal of bloodshed involved.

Famous Folks

The tomb of Cyrus the Great, the founder of the Persian Empire

Additional Layer

This is a painting by Sebastiano Ricci (1708) of Cyrus as an infant being given to a shepherd to kill. Of course, the shepherd and his wife saved the child's life.

Multiculturalism

The first multicultural kingdom on earth was the Persian. Nearly everyone before and since has treated ethic and national groups other than their own with disdain or outright cruelty. The Persians, though, had equal protection under the law thousands of years before Thomas Jefferson.

How do you think the fair laws affected the stability and strength of the Persian Empire?

Called of God?

Cyrus wasn't the only one who believed himself called of God to build a new peaceful empire; the Jews also believed this was the case and their point of view is told in Isaiah 40-55 of the Bible.

Additional Layer

The Persians invented a qanat irrigation system. A deep well is dug into a hill side where the water table in an arid region is closer to the surface. Then a long, horizontal shaft is dug carrying the water long distances to where it is used to irrigate arid land.

of God by Cyrus. Cyrus entered the city of Babylon peacefully and without bloodshed. He restored the temples that had been thrown down by the wicked king of Babylon and freed the slaves. Cyrus declared religious, ethnic, and linguistic equality among all the people of his empire. This cylinder seal has been called the first human rights charter.

" *I am Cyrus, king of the world, great king, mighty king, king of Babylon, king of the land of Sumer and Akkad, king of the four quarters, son of Cambyses, great king, king of Anshan, grandson of Cyrus, great king, king of Anshan, descendant of Teispes, great king, king of Anshan, progeny of an unending royal line, whose rule Bel and Nabu cherish, whose kingship they desire for their hearts' pleasures. When I, well-disposed, entered Babylon, I established the seat of government in the royal palace amidst jubilation and rejoicing. Marduk, the great God, caused the big-hearted inhabitants of Babylon to...me. I sought daily to worship him. My numerous troops moved about undisturbed in the midst of Babylon.*

I did not allow any to terrorize the land of Sumer and Akkad. I kept in view the needs of Babylon and all its sanctuaries to promote their well being. The citizens of Babylon... I lifted their unbecoming yoke. Their dilapidated dwellings I restored. I put an end to their misfortunes. At my deeds Marduk, the great Lord, rejoiced, and to me, Cyrus, the king who worshiped, and to Cambyses, my son, the offspring of my loins, and to all my troops, he graciously gave his blessing, and in good spirit is before him we/glorified/exceedingly his high divinity.

All the kings who sat in the throne rooms, throughout the four quarters, from the Upper to the Lower Sea, those who dwelt in ... all the kings of the West Country who dwelt in tents, brought me their heavy tribute and kissed my feet in Babylon. From ... to the cities of Ashur and Susa, Agade, Eshnuna, the cities of Zamban, Meurnu, Der, as far as the region of the land of Gutium, the holy cities beyond the Tigris whose sanctuaries had been in ruins over a long period, the Gods whose abode is in the midst of them. I returned to the places and housed them in lasting abodes. I gathered together all their inhabitants and restored to them their dwellings. The Gods of Sumer and Akkad whom Nabonidus had, to the anger of the Lord of the Gods, brought into Babylon, I at the bidding of Marduk, the great Lord made to dwell in peace in their habitations, delightful abodes.

May all the gods whom I have placed within their sanctuaries address a daily prayer in my favor before Bel and Nabu, that my days may long, and may they say to Marduk my Lord, May Cyrus the King who reveres thee, and Cambyses his son ..."

Make a time capsule for yourself. First write a lovely letter to the future describing how great and benevolent and wonderful you are, then place it in a metal or plastic container that seals well. Bury it in the back yard for future peoples to find that they may marvel over your magnanimity.

☺ ☻ EXPLORATION: City Planner

Cyrus the Great built a whole new city out of the desert to be his capital. The Persians called it Partha and the Greeks later called it Persepolis. Imagine you were to plan a whole new city. Draw a map of the city you would design. Would it be near water for crops, near the sea for trade, or on a great road? Don't forget to include things like a palace, government buildings, gardens, market place, temples or religious houses, residential areas, craftsmen shops, and more.

Drawing of the palace at Persepolis

☺ ☻ ☻ EXPLORATION: The Great Road

The Persian king built a great road across his empire to speed travel and improve government and trade. The Greek Historian Herodotus wrote about this road. He said:

Now the true account of the road in question is the following:- Royal stations exist along its whole length, and excellent caravanserais; and throughout, it traverses an inhabited tract, and is free from danger. In Lydia and Phrygia there are twenty

Additional Layer

The Old Testament Story, *Daniel and the Lions Den*, features the Persian King Darius. Read and discuss the story from the Bible.

Daniel in the Lions Den by Peter Paul Rubens (1615)

Additional Layer

When the Persians invaded Greece, they were defeated at Marathon, a city in northern Greece.

A soldier named Pheidippides ran and carried the news of the victory to Athens, over 20 miles, and we now have long races called marathons because of this event. Legend has it that he delivered his message: "Niki!" (which means "victory") and then died right then and there.

Find out more about the traditions of marathon races since then. When did the first modern marathon take place? When was the distance changed to 26.2 miles, and why?

stations within a distance Of 94 ½ parasangs. On leaving Phrygia the Halys has to be crossed; and here are gates through which you must needs pass ere you can traverse the stream. A strong force guards this post. When you have made the passage, and are come into Cappadocia, 28 stations and 104 parasangs bring you to the borders of Cilicia, where the road passes through two sets of gates, at each of which there is a guard posted. Leaving these behind, you go on through Cilicia, where you find three stations in a distance of 15 ½ parasangs. The boundary between Cilicia and Armenia is the river Euphrates, which it is necessary to cross in boats. In Armenia the resting-places are 15 in number, and the distance is 56 ½ parasangs. There is one place where a guard is posted. Four large streams intersect this district, all of which have to be crossed by means of boats. The first of these is the Tigris; the second and the third have both of them the same name, though they are not only different rivers, but do not even run from the same place. For the one which I have called the first of the two has its source in Armenia, while the other flows afterwards out of the country of the Matienians. The fourth of the streams is called the Gyndes, and this is the river which Cyrus dispersed by digging for it three hundred and sixty channels. Leaving Armenia and entering the Matienian country, you have four stations; these passed you find yourself in Cissia, where eleven stations and 42 ½ parasangs bring you to another navigable stream, the Choaspes, on the banks of which the city of Susa is built. Thus the entire number of the stations is raised to one hundred and eleven; and so many are in fact the resting-places that one finds between Sardis and Susa.

After you have read the description of the road, draw it on a map of the "Ancient Middle East", at the end of this unit. Include the stations and river crossings, the walls and the guards. Add in rivers that are described.

☺ ☻ EXPLORATION: The Evil King Darius?

Herodotus also told many stories about Darius, the Persian King. When you read the stories, which Herodotus heard as rumors from other people, you have to remember that the Greeks hated the Persians. Do you think the following story is true? Maybe it is, maybe it is only partly true, or maybe it is completely false. Re-write the story as a picture book for kids (A gruesome picture book).

The preparations of Darius against the Scythians had begun, messengers had been despatched on all sides with the king's commands, some being required to furnish troops, others to supply ships, others again to bridge the Thracian Bosphorus, when Artabanus, son of Hystaspes and brother of Darius, entreated the king to desist from his expedition, urging on him the great difficulty of attacking Scythia. Good, however, as the advice of Artabanus was, it failed to persuade Darius. He therefore ceased his reasonings; and Darius, when his preparations were complete, led his army forth from Susa.

It was then that a certain Persian, by name Oeobazus, the father of three sons, all of whom were to accompany the army, came and prayed the king that he would allow one of his sons to remain with him. Darius made answer, as if he regarded him in the light of a friend who had urged a moderate request, "that he would allow them all to remain." Oeobazus was overjoyed, expecting that all his children would be excused from serving; the king, however, bade his attendants take the three sons of Oeobazus and forthwith put them to death. Thus they were all left behind, but not till they had been deprived of life.

King Darius Meeting with Scythian Emissaries, painting by Polish artist Pranciškus Smuglevičius (c. 1875)

☺ ☻ EXPLORATION: A Bridge of Boats

After a terrible defeat at Marathon, the Persians prepared to fight back. They began carrying in supplies and building bridges to cross the Hellespont, a narrow strait that connects the Aegean Sea to the Sea of Marmara. After storms wiped out their bridges, they decided on a new game plan. They lashed boats together, creating a bridge made of boats that they used to cross over on to the Greek mainland. They marched on to Greece and defeated the Greek stronghold of Athens.

Excavations of ancient shipyards from that area have revealed that many of their warships were just 6 meters wide. The span of the water ranges from 1.2 to 6 kilometers wide. Can you figure out the minimum number of ships they would have had to lash together to complete their ship bridge and make it across?

Look up the Hellespont on a map and draw a diagram of what the bridge would have looked like.

☺ ☻ ☻ EXPLORATION: The Persian Times

Pretend you are a reporter getting information for a story you are writing on the defeat of the Persians at Plataea. Answer the essential questions in your article: Who? What? Where? When? Why? How? Write an article in standard newspaper format and include drawings of maps and sketches of the battle scene. Use the newspaper template from the printables at www.layers-of-learning.com to create your front page of The Persian Times.

GEOGRAPHY: ARCTIC & ANTARCTIC

The polar regions, both Arctic and Antarctic, are places too cold to support the growth of trees, including areas of ice caps and tundra. The tops of high mountains above the tree line also have a similar climate, but these areas are known as alpine climates. The climate of the poles due to their location in the high latitudes, furthest from the equator. They receive less direct sunlight than most of the planet. Furthermore, the ice and snow in these areas reflect much of the little sunlight they get, making it even colder.

These cold climates, sometimes called frigid zones, have very short summers in general and a low amount of precipitation. In tundra areas, mostly to the north, grasses and low bushes grow furiously in the approximately eight weeks of summer. And coyotes, wolves, foxes, bears, rodents, birds, and insects furiously eat and grow to store up for the long winter. The birds migrate south to warmer regions for the winter.

In areas covered with ice caps, life centers on the sea. The few birds and mammals who live there feed on fish and other sea creatures. The North Pole is covered by pack ice that floats over the Arctic Ocean. The South Pole has the continent of Antarctica situated atop it; it is also covered by ice.

☺ ☻ EXPLORATION: Mapping the Arctic
Use the map of the Arctic with grid lines found in the printables. Map these locations using latitude and longitude. Make note of how latitude and longitude look very different on a map centered on the North Pole than they do on a map centered on the equator.

North Pole	90° N
Magnetic North Pole	82.7°N 114.4°W (it moves though, check for the latest)
Prudhoe Bay, AK	70°19′32″N 148°42′41″W
Barrow, AK	71°17′44″N 156°45′59″W
Inuvik,Can	68°21′42″N 133°43′50″W
Alert, Can	82°30′05″N 062°20′20″W
Pevek, Rus	69°42′00″N 170°17′00″E
Tiksi, Rus	71°38′N 128°52′E
Murmansk, Rus	68°58′N 33°05′E
Noril'sk, Rus	69°20′N 88°13′E
Daneborg, Gre	74°18′N 20°14′W
Longyearbyen, Nor	78°14′17″N 15°26′50″E
Savissivik, Gre	76°01′10″N 65°06′50″W

Additional Layer
The north pole is sea, nearly completely surrounded by land. The south pole is a massive continent surrounded by sea. The south is much colder than the north. Why do you think there is such a difference?

Fabulous Fact
Arctic zones can be defined by the arctic circle, by temperature, or by the tree line. There's no absolute agreement about where the arctic zone really is.

Additional Layer
The arctic regions are heavily distorted on flat maps of the world. Show your kids a map of the North and South Pole or use a globe to see the area in a less distorted version. Explain how various types of map projections (Unit 1-1) are best for different types of maps. Particularly compare Greenland to Africa on a flat map of the world and using a globe.

Additional Layer

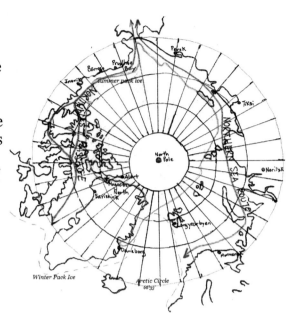

The Earth has a magnetic field surrounding it and concentrating at the poles. Scientists believe the magnetic field is responsible for the auroras and for animal migration. We know the magnetic field aids us in navigation with a compass, essential to polar explorations of the past two centuries. You can learn more about magnets in Unit 2-19.

Riddle

If you build a house with four walls and four windows, one in each wall, and all the windows face south, where are you?

North Pole

On the Web

Visit http://www.fourmilab.ch/earthview/vplanet.html and click on "map of the Earth". Then reset the latitude to 90° N. You will see a live satellite view of how the Earth actually looks from the North Pole at the present moment.

Then trace the permanent ice cap region in blue and the northern shipping route in red. These shipping routes are potential routes, not ones that are actually used, as there is too much sea ice to make them practical. If the globe does warm though, they may be used in the future, greatly reducing shipping times between the Atlantic and Pacific Oceans.

☺ **EXPLORATION: Arctic Map**
Color the second, simpler "North Polar Region" map found at the end of this unit. Put a red dot at each town and trace the shipping route in red. Color the permanent ice cap white, the winter ice pack light blue, the seas dark blue, and the tundra purple. There's quite a seasonal change in the amount of ice at the poles.

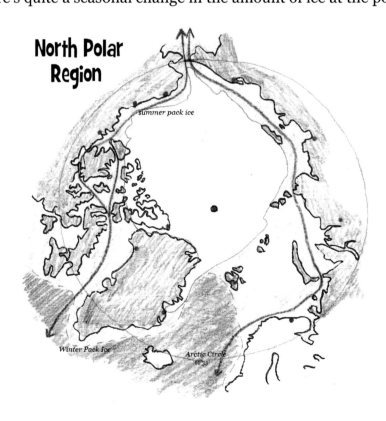

Again, the marked shipping routes on the map are potential, not actually used, because the ice conditions in the Arctic Ocean would make it dangerous for ships to navigate through.

☺ ☻ EXPLORATION: Arctic Animal

Choose one of these animals that lives in a northern polar region and learn more about it. What does it need to survive in the cold? Does it migrate in the winter? What does it eat? Is it endangered?

Polar Bear
Arctic Tern
Musk Ox
Reindeer
Arctic Fox
Snowy Owl
Humpback Whale
Arctic Hare

Write a report and presented in a creative way and share it with an audience. You can find a template for the polar bear report at the end of this unit or on the printables page at Layers-of-Learning.com

☺ ☻ EXPLORATION: Antarctic Animal

Now choose an animal that lives in the southern polar region and learn more about it. Go online and find a how-to-draw tutorial on your animal, then surround your drawing with all the information you find about the species on a poster. Specifically, find out what makes your species well suited for life in such a harsh environment.

Additional Layer

The polar regions haven't always been so cold. Scientists have found fossils of warm weather plants and animals above the Arctic circle and in Greenland. Even in perpetually frozen Antarctica there used to be tundra plants and animals. Look it up.

Photo by Broken Inaglory, CC

Fabulous Facts

The North and South Poles have latitude coordinates (90° N and S, respectively), but no longitude coordinates. They also have no time zone. Scientists who work in these areas just use Greenwich mean time.

Famous Folks

Ernest Shackleton was another failed explorer like Robert Scott, but though he never reached his goal at the South Pole, he miraculously made it out of the Antarctic with every member of his team after repeated hardships. Read about him in *Shipwreck at the Bottom of the World* by Jennifer Armstrong.

Here are a few ideas of Antarctic animals to choose from:
- Penguins (choose a specific species)
- Seals (again, there are many kinds)
- Whales
- Krill
- Albatross
- Snow petrels

If you want to focus on penguins, you should check out *March of the Penguins*. It's one of the best animal documentaries I've ever seen.

☺ ☻ ☻ EXPLORATION: Famous Features of Antarctica

Using a student atlas and the Antarctic Polar Region map at the end of this unit, color a map of Antarctica including these locations:
- South Pole
- Amundsen Sea
- Weddell Sea
- Ross Sea
- Lazarev Sea
- Palmer Land
- Wilkes Land
- Enderby Land
- Marie Byrd Land
- Dronning Maud Land
- Bellingshausen Sea

Search the internet for information about each of the people these features are named for. Print out small images of the people and glue them to the map at the feature named after them. For younger kids this may be too many people to research. Just choose four or five of the people to learn about.

☺ ☻ EXPLORATION: Temperature Difference

Make three thermometers from construction paper. Use a background paper that is any color other than red. Draw three rectangles on your background paper, 1" wide and as tall as will fit on your paper (I traced a ruler for my rectangles). Now mark your rectangles in 1 cm increments. Label the marks starting at the bottom with -120° F and moving up in 10 degree increments until you reach 120°F.

Look up today's high temperature at the North Pole, the South Pole and your hometown.

Cut three long strips of red construction paper 1" wide . Trim each rectangle of red to match your thermometer scale to show the temperature at each location. Write each temperature in bold on each thermometer. Label the thermometers with the location and temperature. Label the paper with the date.

As you work, talk about why the poles are colder than other places on Earth:

- The Sun does not hit the poles directly, but at a steep angle. This spreads the rays out over a much larger area, meaning that the same amount of energy is spread more thinly.
- The Sun's rays, at this greater angle, travel through more of the Earth's atmosphere than closer to the equator. The atmosphere reflects much of the Sun's heat; more atmosphere means less sunlight gets through.
- Much of the Sun's heat is reflected off the white snow, an effect called albedo.
- For part of the year, the Sun doesn't hit the poles at all, meaning a deep cold period, which freezes ice and ground, carrying over the cold into the sunny season as well. This happens because of the Earth's tilt, the same reason we have seasonal changes in most parts of the world.

☺ ☻ EXPLORATION: People of the Poles

Nobody really lives south of the Antarctic Circle, but scientists have permanent bases there and ecotourists visit Antarctica in the summer months. There's even a marathon held in Antarctica every year.

But people really do live above the Arctic Circle in the north. Some of these groups include the Inuit of North America, the Sami of Scandinavia, and the Yugyt and Nenet of Siberia. In the past these people were all nomadic, living largely off the sea, but today many of them have moved into towns in the far north.

How do people survive in places that are so cold year round?

Writer's Workshop

Choose one of the Antarctic explorers and write an obituary about them. You may want to pull out your local newspaper and read a few obituaries so you can mimic the proper format.

Fabulous Facts

Some Antarctic distances:

The continent is 5.4 million square miles, quite a bit bigger than Europe or the US.

The United States is 3.6 million square miles.

It's 9,920 miles from Washington D.C. to McMurdo Station, Antarctica.

Additional Layer

One of the huge difficulties that has arisen from the Antarctic Research Stations is the pollution and garbage that is piling up there. For the tiny population, there is quite a bit of trash.

Explanation

The one thing that is a bigger influence in the education of children than anything else is the level of their mom's education.

When I use the word "education" I do not mean how many years of schooling mom received or the grades she got. Education is much more than schooling. It occurs everywhere that life happens. It happens in the classroom, but it also happens in the garden, at the grocery store, in the bank, at the real estate office, on the couch with a good book, in the garage under the hood of a car, and in front of the TV.

So the degree to which Mom is engaged in and curious about the world is the degree to which her children will be.

Be involved in learning hands-on. Plant a garden if you never have, take the music lessons you always wanted to, spend time in nature just really seeing for the first time everything that's been in front of your eyes all along. And read, read, read.

Michelle

What do they eat? What are their houses like? What kinds of clothes do they wear? Do they drive cars, shop in grocery stores, and go to school nowadays?

Choose one of these groups of people and create a diorama that showcases their lifestyle and environment. Use a shoebox and create a scene that shows their home and other interesting things you discover.

☺ ☻ **EXPLORATION: Cool Research Expedition**
You are a scientist. Make plans for your upcoming expedition to Palmer Station in Antarctica. You will need to 1.) plan how to get there, 2.) decide what supplies you will need, and 3.) determine what scientific research you'd like to do while there.

Planning how to get there might be tricky. You can't fly into Palmer without a ski-equipped plane, so you'll probably need to take a boat from Punta Arenas, Chile. Plan out and map your air travel from your hometown to Punta Arenas, and then map your ship travel aboard the *Laurence M. Gould* ship that sails to Palmer Station.

Refer to the USAP Participant Guide at www.usap.gov to help you decide what you will pack for your trip. It's a guide put together by the United States Antarctic Program to help people prepare for a scientific expedition there. You are only allowed to take 2 70-pound packs with you to Antarctica, so you won't be able to take everything. Refer to the lists from the guide and make your own "to-pack" list. To involve some math, write the approximate weight of each item and then add up your items to make sure you are within the weight limit (the backpack itself could weigh up to 5 pounds without anything in it!).

Ernest Shakleton, Robert Scott, and Edward Wilson of the British Discovery Expedition, 1902

Once you arrive you've got to have a research plan. Palmer Station is situated right near several penguin colonies, so a lot of the research there centers around Antarctic wildlife and marine biology. You may want to read the Wikipedia article about Palmer Station for more ideas about what you could research. Here are a few topics to consider: ozone changes, climatology, glaciology, astronomy, marine ecosystems, and marine biology. Write down your research topic and some questions you want to answer while you're there.

Now put together all your plans and bind them into your own Antarctic travel plan book.

EXPLANATION: Polar Regions on Pinterest

Find even more activities and lesson plans on the Layers of Learning Geography – Polar Regions Pinterest Board. You'll find more learning fun for kids of all ages – everything from arctic animal art and fun snack ideas to the volcanic activity of Antarctica.
http://www.pinterest.com/layerslearning/geography-polar-regions/

Geography - Polar Regions

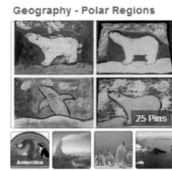

Additional Layer
The Antarctic Treaty outlines that no nation can own Antarctica. It has been signed by 45 countries and says that although no one owns the land, it can be used for scientific research by all. It is a peaceful land, dedicated to science. There cannot be any military presence or structures there. Besides all nations being allowed to research there, the scientists from around the world share their research findings with the other treaty nations.

On the Web
There's a great educational site by Berkeley about the Northern and Southern lights for kids. It's called *Auroras: Mysterious Lights in the Sky*. Just google "berkeley auroras" and you'll find it.

It explains the where and why of the auroras and has lots of great fact sheets at the end.

SCIENCE: WAVES

Fabulous Fact

Some physical waves include earthquakes, water waves, sound waves, a playground swing, a bouncing trampoline . . . and this wave:

Fabulous Fact

Electromagnetic waves include x-rays, radio waves, television, visible light, and microwaves.

Fabulous Fact

Values in physics are given Greek letters to designate them.

Wavelength is given the Greek symbol lambda, λ.

A wave is a transference of energy from one point to another. Sometimes it can be seen as a pendulum swinging back and forth, other times it is like a flowing up and down motion, and in still other cases it is simply a vibration passed from one particle to another. There are two major types of waves: mechanical and electromagnetic. Mechanical waves travel through a physical medium like air, water, or earth. Electromagnetic waves can travel without physical substance to travel through, like light waves traveling through space.

The speed the wave oscillates at is called its frequency. Everything has a natural frequency, it will vibrate if set in motion. The top of a wave is called the crest and the bottom of the wave is called the trough. The amplitude of the wave is the height of the wave from the bottom of the trough to the top of the crest.

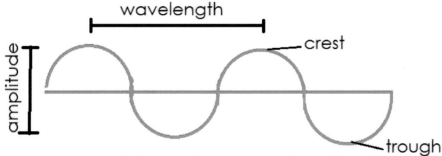

Frequency is how often a wavelength passes in a given amount of time.

☺ ☺ ☺ **EXPERIMENT: Waves**

Use a rope, like a jump rope, to demonstrate waves. You need two people, one to hold each end. Move your hands up and down to create waves along the rope. Define the different parts of a wave and which type of wave you have created: Crest, trough, mechanical wave. Can you adjust the amplitude?

☺ ☺ ☻ EXPERIMENT: Pendulum Waves

Show pendulum waves with a backyard or playground swing. Have one child sit on the swing and slowly swing back and forth without pumping. Time how long each oscillation is from when the swing is in its furthest forward position until it returns to that same position. Now try timing the swinger when he is going higher. What is the oscillation speed now? How does it compare to the slower swinger?

☺ ☻ EXPERIMENT: Moving Energy

Waves move energy from place to place, but they do not move the physical substance much. Try this experiment to demonstrate: Float a cork or a piece of Styrofoam, on water in a filled sink or a plastic tub. Make a wave by touching the surface of the water in an up and down motion. The wave will move along the water surface, but the cork will only bob up and down. Try it again, this time use a straw and blow across the surface of the water, like wind whipping up waves on the ocean or in a lake. What happens to your piece of cork?

If you blow across the water or make a side to side wave, you are using forces other than wave motion so your cork will move, but still most of the energy is transferred along with the wave, the water itself isn't moving much.

☺ ☺ ☻ EXPERIMENT: Energy Transfer

You need five marbles of the same size. Line four of them up along a smooth surface. Gently roll the fifth marble into one end of the line. Observe what happens to all the marbles. The one on the far end should move, but the others remain in place. The energy is transferred along the line of marbles. This is how energy is transferred through waves as well.

Explanation

Think about a buoy in the ocean. The buoy moves up and down with the wave as it passes, but is not moved side to side.

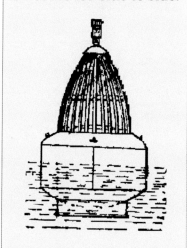

Additional Layer

The oldest known marbles were found in the Indus river valley Mohenjo-daro excavation and were at least 4000 years old.

Learn more about the history and manufacture of marbles.

Additional Layer
Remember the old tin-can telephone? It uses the principles of waves, transferred from the air to the string and back to the air, to work. Make one.

Additional Layer

If a tree falls in a forest and no one is around to hear it does it make a sound?

Photograph by Chris Reynolds

This is both a physics and a logic question. It all depends on how you define your terms. What is sound?

If sound is vibration in air then, yes, a tree falling all by its lonesome still makes a sound.

But if sound is the effect of vibrations on an ear-drum or recording equipment then no, the lonesome falling tree makes no sound.

Precisely defining terms is an important part of both science and logic.

☺ ☺ ☻ **EXPLORATION: Bridge Collapse**
Look up the "Tacoma Bridge Collapse" on You Tube. There are some great videos of the natural frequency of this bridge oscillating in the wind. The natural frequency of the bridge was one oscillation every five seconds. The oscillations got larger, but the frequency stayed the same until the bridge collapsed. That means that the waves got more violent as the bridge kept oscillating, but the speed stayed one oscillation for every five seconds.

☺ ☺ ☻ **EXPERIMENT: Sound Waves**
Sound waves travel with compression, rather than an up and down motion like water waves. The energy of the sound wave can be carried over very long distances but the air molecules themselves don't move much. Demonstrate this with a Slinky. With two people, stretch out the Slinky with one person holding each end. Use a quick motion to "shove" the slinky toward your partner followed immediately by a rapid pull. Watch as the compression wave travels between the two people.

☺ ☻ **EXPERIMENT: Pitch**
Fill three glasses with water. One should be full nearly to the top, one about halfway and the last only an inch or so. Now tap the edge of the glass with a spoon. You can hear different pitches. The most full glass will have the deepest sound, while the least full will have the highest.

The sound is higher or lower because of oscillation speed. Low sounds are oscillating at a lower speed than high sounds. The amount of water in the glass changes the oscillation speed of the sound waves coming from it when tapped.

Fill eight or so glasses at different amounts and then put them in order of pitch. Try playing a little tune like *Mary Had A Little Lamb*.

☺ ☻ **EXPERIMENT: Ear-drum**
We can hear because of sound waves bouncing off our ear drums. To see how this works, get a wide-mouthed glass bowl and stretch plastic wrap across it very tightly. It must be tight or this will not work.

Now toss a few grains of rice into the middle of the plastic wrap. Bang a pot loudly very near to the bowl and watch the rice jiggle and move as the sound vibrates the plastic wrap. Have the kids make other noises and yell near it to get it to move also. This is how your eardrum works as well.

☺ ☻ ☻ **EXPERIMENT: Light waves**

Light waves have the ability to transfer energy without "stuff" for it to travel through, but they still act as waves in many ways. They can cancel each other out or amplify each other, just like other types of waves. Try the classic two slit experiment. Using a piece of dark construction paper, cut parallel narrow slits in the paper about 3 inches long and two inches apart. Go into a darkened room and shine a flashlight through the slits onto a wall. Adjust the distance between the paper and the light until you can see a pattern of many parallel lines on the wall. The light particles are canceling each other out (dark bars) in some spots and amplifying each other (light bars) in others.

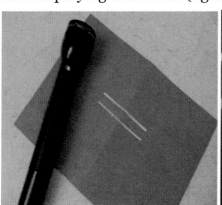

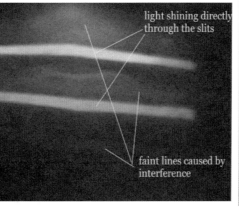

light shining directly through the slits

faint lines caused by interference

Fabulous Fact
For years scientists debated about whether light was a wave or a particle. They finally threw up their hands and decided it was both. It was our friend, Albert Einstein, who first proposed that light could have a dual nature. Darn it! That's not tidy; and scientists since Newton have always believed in nice, tidy mathematical packages. Einstein really threw more than the laws of motion on its head.

Additional Layer
Metaphorically speaking, "light" is usually seen as "good" while "darkness" is "bad". Think of some examples.

Famous Folks
Thomas Young first demonstrated the classic two-slit experiment showing the canceling effects of light waves. His experiments proved once and for all that light does behave as a wave.

Painting by Sir Thomas Lawrence

THE ARTS: MELODY IN MUSIC

Additional Layer

Young Flute Player by Judith Leyster

Favorite American Melodies

Home on the Range

America the Beautiful

Buffalo Gals

Skip To My Loo

Camptown Races

Oh, Susanna

Over the Rainbow

Lavender's Blue

Yankee Doodle

Battle Hymn of the Republic

I've Been Workin' On the Railroad

The Yellow Rose of Texas

Anchor's Aweigh

You can find the music and lyrics to all of these songs online.

Melody in music is the combination of pitch and rhythm. It's the musical line that you hear, play, or sing to in a song. We begin learning simple melodies at very young ages. *Twinkle, Twinkle, Little Star* may just be one of the most famous American melodies — almost anyone can recognize it whether it is sung or played on the piano, a xylophone, a trumpet, or an electric guitar. All of these instruments sound very different, but they can play the very same melody. We depend on instruments (or voices) to hear a melody.

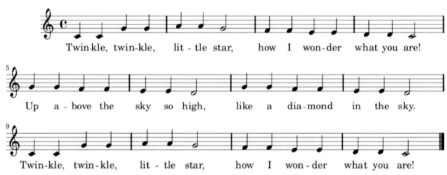

Twinkle Twinkle Little Star

Melodies usually have phrases, much like we have sentences and phrases when we speak. They are like musical thoughts that have pauses, louder and softer sections, quick and slow parts, and different tones and feelings.

The very best way to learn about notes and melody is to learn to play an instrument. By learning an instrument you not only learn the direct skills it takes to play it, but you also can't help but learn a great deal of musical theory along the way.

☺ ☺ ☺ **EXPLORATION: Instrument Families**
Unlike rhythm, melody requires pitch. If you beat out the rhythm of *Twinkle, Twinkle Little Star*, you likely won't be able to recognize it at all. We depend on the highness and lowness of the notes, or pitch, for melody. Because of this, you can't just create the sound randomly. Musical instruments have to be perfectly tuned to have the right pitch. Learn which instruments belong to which family of instruments, and then play this game of instrument tag for some practice.

Call out a family of instruments. The person who is "It" tags someone and they become "It." Here's the catch-- if the kid can name an instrument in that family before they are tagged, they get to sit down, making them safe from being tagged. They only get to sit for 10 seconds, then they have to rejoin the game. They can't use the same instrument more than once. When you call out a new family, they have to use instruments from the new family. Here are the basics, though there are many more unique instruments out there, so this list is not exhaustive:

Library
Visit the Library CD section and pick out various styles of music to listen to.

Strings: the strings are plucked or bowed
- violin
- viola
- cello
- bass
- harp
- guitar

Woodwinds: air is blown inside. The sound happens from the vibrations caused by the blown air (wind).
- flute
- oboe
- clarinet
- bassoon
- contrabassoon
- piccolo
- English horn
- saxophone
- recorder

Brass: made of brass and make sound when air is blown inside.
- trumpet
- trombone
- tuba
- french horn

Percussion: they are struck or shaken
- cymbals
- timpani
- roto-toms
- tam-tam
- tubular bells
- glockenspiels
- vibraphone
- maracas
- tambourines
- triangle
- chimes

Keyboard Instruments: all of these have a keyboard that creates the sound when keys are pressed.
- piano
- grand piano
- celesta
- harpsichord
- organ
- synthesizer

Voice: This is a unique instrument because it is within us. We can create melodies and sounds with the air inside our bodies.
- You!

☺ ☻ **EXPLORATION: Name That Tune**
Using familiar recorded songs, play just a few bars to the kids. (If you don't play an instrument, you can play the CD player.) This works really well if you have a selection of children's music. They try to figure out the song before anyone else. You could all sing the songs when they guess correctly.

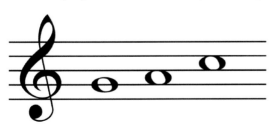

Juan Gris, *Guitar and Pipe*, 1913

Famous Folks

Stephen Foster is an American composer who wrote many of the songs we now consider to be American folk songs like *Oh, Susanna, Beautiful Dreamer*, and *Swanee River*.

Additional Layer

Peter and the Wolf by Sergei Prokofiev was written for children to introduce them to the instruments of the orchestra. Each character is represented by a different instrument as follows:

Bird: flute
Duck: oboe
Cat: clarinet
Grandfather: bassoon
Wolf: French horns
Hunters: woodwind theme, with gunshots on timpani and bass drum
Peter: string instruments

Listen to it (or watch it in one of many video forms) with your kids.

☺ ☺ Exploration: Highs and Lows

Play a piece of familiar music with a simple melody line. Children's music CDs are perfect for this. As it goes along, raise your hand higher when the pitch goes up, and go lower as the pitch goes down. Many people who teach children to sing actually use this technique as they are directing to help kids visually see where their voices need to go as they sing. Sing along as you raise and lower the pitch with your hand.

☺ ☺ EXPEDITION: Music Store

A music store is the perfect place to see instruments close up. If it's not too busy and you ask for a tour they'll likely even let you try your hand at playing some of the instruments.

☺ ☺ EXPLORATION: Listen By Instrument

Go visit www.dsokids.com and click on listen, then in the drop down menu, select instrument. You'll see a big list of instruments to choose from. Each instrument will play so you can hear its sound. It will also play *Twinkle, Twinkle Little Star* for you. You can turn it into a guessing game and try to figure out which instrument is playing just by listening.

☺ EXPLORATION: Moving To The Melody

This is a chance for kids to move while listening to melodies within music. Get some fun-to-dance-to songs and play Freeze Dance. The kids dance and move as long as the song is playing, but when the music stops they immediately have to FREEZE! You can incorporate tempo by including slower and faster songs and showing them how they move slowly to songs with a slow tempo and quickly to songs with a fast tempo.

☺ ☺ EXPEDITION: Concert

Find out when and where there is a musical concert or recital near you. Local middle schools, high schools, universities, music stores, theaters, and music schools are great places to ask.

☺ ☺ ☺ EXPLORATION: Mmm Mmm Melody

To help kids learn how notes are placed on the staff, have them put M&Ms on staff paper, which you'll find in the printables. Demonstrate how the notes can be line notes (placed so the M&M is being bisected by the line) or space notes (the M&M fits in between 2 lines). After they've placed their M&M's you may want to play their melody if you're able to read music. At the very least, you could demonstrate how the notes go up when they go higher on the staff, and go lower when the notes are placed lower.

You can write your own musical phrases or try to create the melody of a song you know on the staff. We've included a longer staff page at the end of the unit as well for kids who want to write an actual song.

As notes go higher on the staff, the pitch goes up. This is the first line of Mary Had A Little Lamb. Can you follow along the pitches as you sing it?

☺ ☻ EXPLORATION: Scribble Melody

Give everyone a piece of paper and a pile of crayons. Close your eyes and start some music. Scribble along to the music. If the music is soft and slow the crayons will move slowly and gently; if the music is fast and loud the crayons will go like crazy! Every so often you call out "SWITCH!" Switch colors and keep going!

Additional Layer

Just like books, music has categories or types of music. The three major categories are:

Art: Music produced in a formal or classical style.

Popular: Music easily accessible for the people. This is what you hear on the radio.

Traditional: This is another way of saying "folk music"

There are subcategories of music as well. For instance jazz, rock 'n roll, and country music are very different from each other, but they are all under the major category of popular music.

Listen to lots of different types of music. Learn what you like and what you don't and try to figure out why you feel the way you do. This will help you learn to have a trained ear.

Coming up next:

Unit 1-10

Ancient China
Forests – Machines
Chinese Art

My Ideas For This Unit:

Title: _____   Topic: _____

_____

_____

_____

_____

_____

_____

_____

_____

_____

_____

Title: _____   Topic: _____

_____

_____

_____

_____

_____

_____

_____

_____

_____

_____

_____

_____

Title: _____   Topic: _____

_____

_____

_____

_____

_____

_____

_____

_____

_____

PERSIANS – ARCTIC – WAVES – MELODY

My Ideas For This Unit:

Title: _____   Topic: _____

_____

_____

_____

_____

_____

_____

_____

_____

_____

Title: _____   Topic: _____

_____

_____

_____

_____

_____

_____

_____

_____

_____

Title: _____   Topic: _____

_____

_____

_____

_____

_____

_____

_____

_____

The Tomb of Cyrus The Great

Cyrus the Great was the founder of the Persian Empire. By conquering other nations, but allowing them to keep their own cultures while paying him tribute, he expanded his wealth and territory very quickly. He also freed slaves in all the lands he captured. He was buried in a tomb. Inside there was a golden bed, a table set up with drinking cups, a gold coffin, and some ornaments with precious stones. When the Islamic people conquered the region they wanted to destroy the tomb. The people convinced them that it was not the tomb of Cyrus, but was where Solomon's mother was buried. The inscription was changed and it is still known as the tomb of the mother of Solomon.

Persia: Unit I-9

1300 BC I-9

Medes in the north and Persians in the south settle into cities

728-330BC I-9

Dynasty of the Medes

700-600 BC I-9

The kingdom of Edia and the kingdom of Persia are set up

559-530 BC I-9

Cyrus II (the great) is king of Persia

550 BC I-9

Cyrus defeats the Medes

522-486 BC I-9

Darius I is king of Persia and the empire reaches its greatest extent

486-465 BC I-9

Greeks and Persians go to war

486-465 BC I-9

Xerxes I, son of Darius, is king of Persia

331-330 BC I-9

Persia is conquered by Alexander the Great

330-312 BC I-9

Hellenistic Dynasty

312-238 BC I-9

Seleucid Dynasty

238BC-224AD I-9

Parthian Dynasty

123−87 BC I-9

Mithradates II (the Great) rules

224−651 AD I-9

Sassanian Dynasty

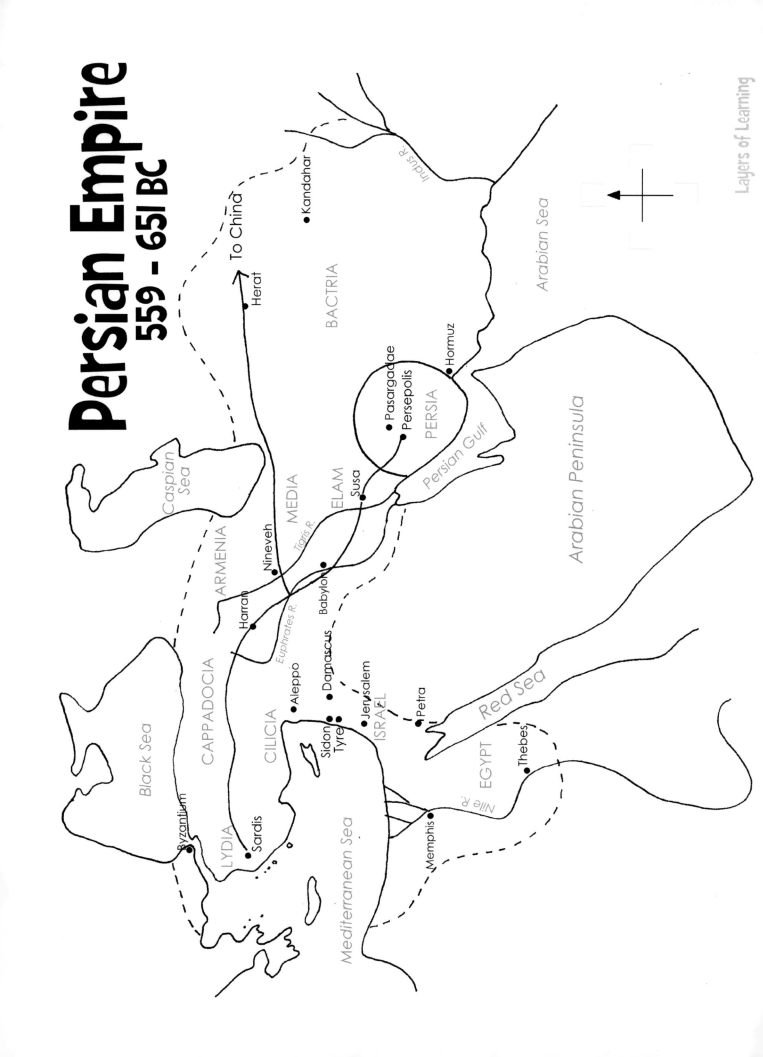

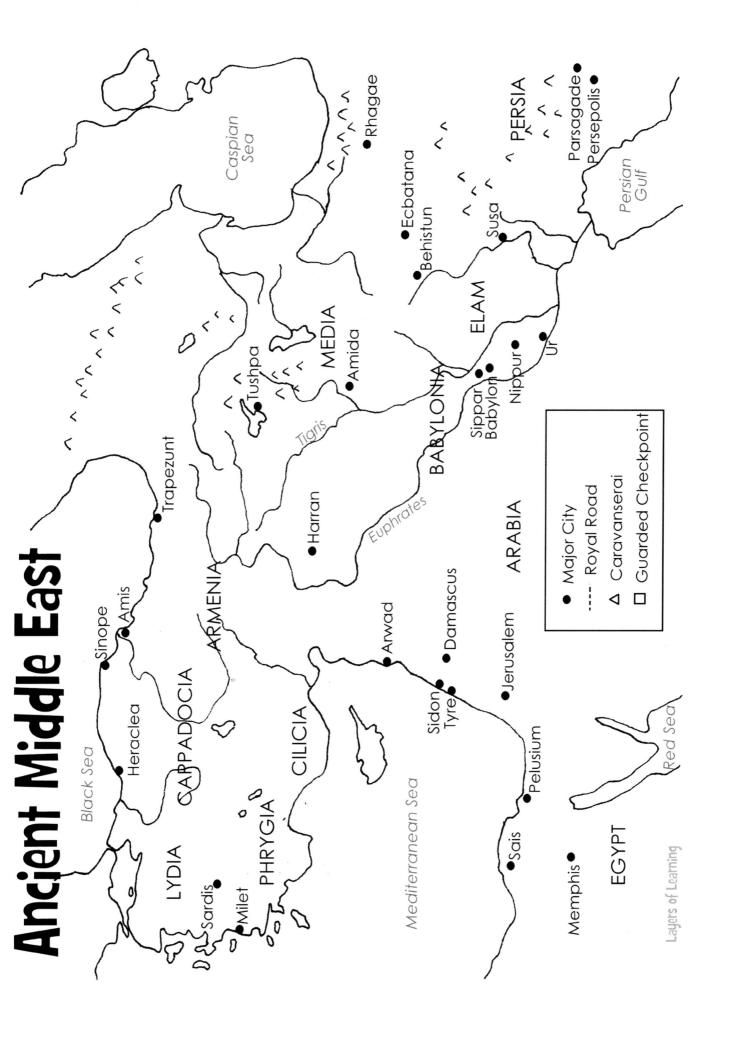

Ancient Middle East

Caspian Sea

Rhagae

PERSIA

Parsagade
Persepolis

Ecbatana
Behistun

Susa

ELAM

Persian Gulf

MEDIA

Amida

Tushpa

Tigris

BABYLONIA

Sippar
Babylon
Nippur
Ur

Harran

Euphrates

ARABIA

Trapezunt

ARMENIA

Arwad

Damascus

Jerusalem

Sinope
Amis

Heraclea

CAPPADOCIA

CILICIA

Sidon
Tyre

Black Sea

LYDIA

PHRYGIA

Sardis
Milet

Mediterranean Sea

Pelusium

Sais

Memphis

EGYPT

Red Sea

- Major City
--- Royal Road
△ Caravanserai
□ Guarded Checkpoint

North Polar Region

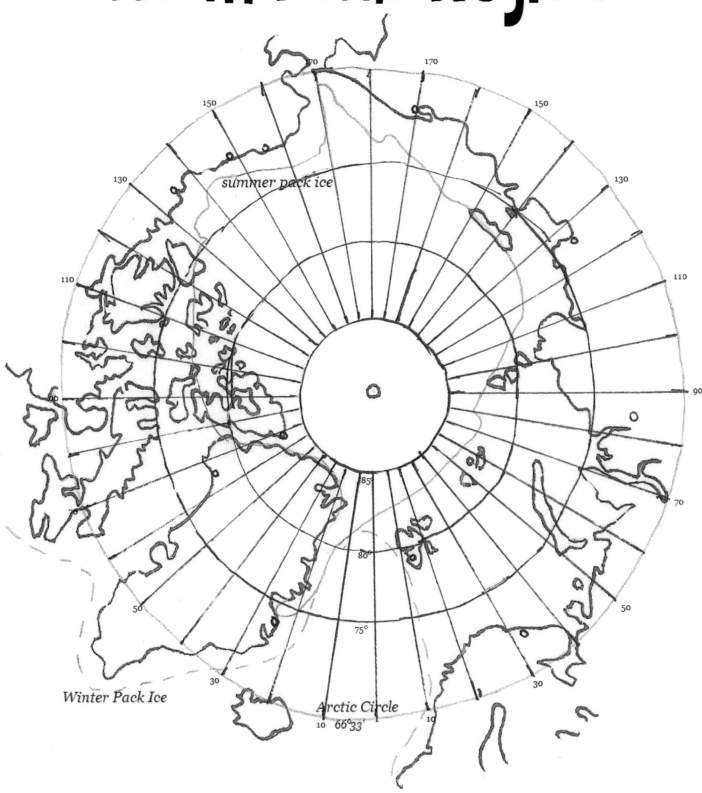

North Polar Region

summer pack ice

Winter Pack Ice

Arctic Circle
66°33'

Antarctic Polar Region

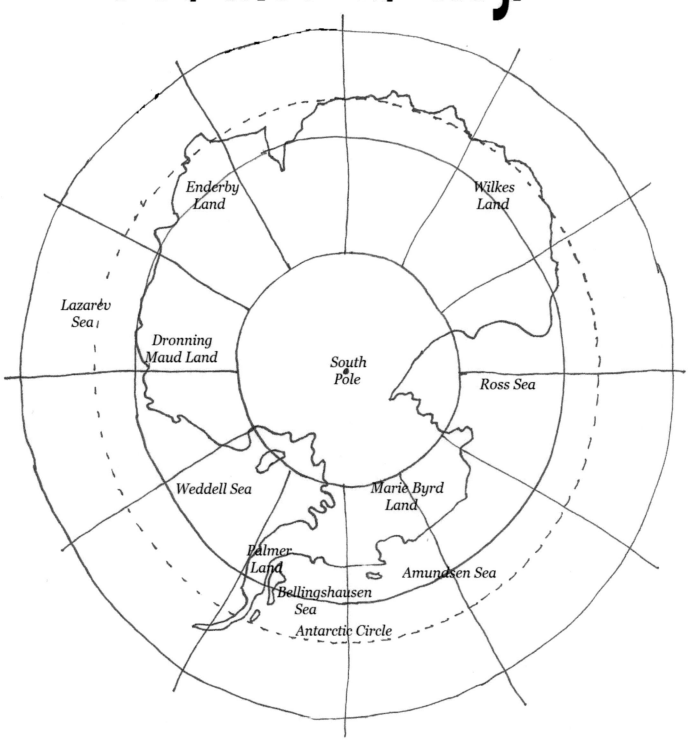

Enderby Land

Wilkes Land

Lazarev Sea

Dronning Maud Land

South Pole

Ross Sea

Weddell Sea

Marie Byrd Land

Palmer Land

Amundsen Sea

Bellingshausen Sea

Antarctic Circle

Polar Bear Report

Cut out the polar bear
pieces and attach them
to a piece of report paper
to write about polar bears on.

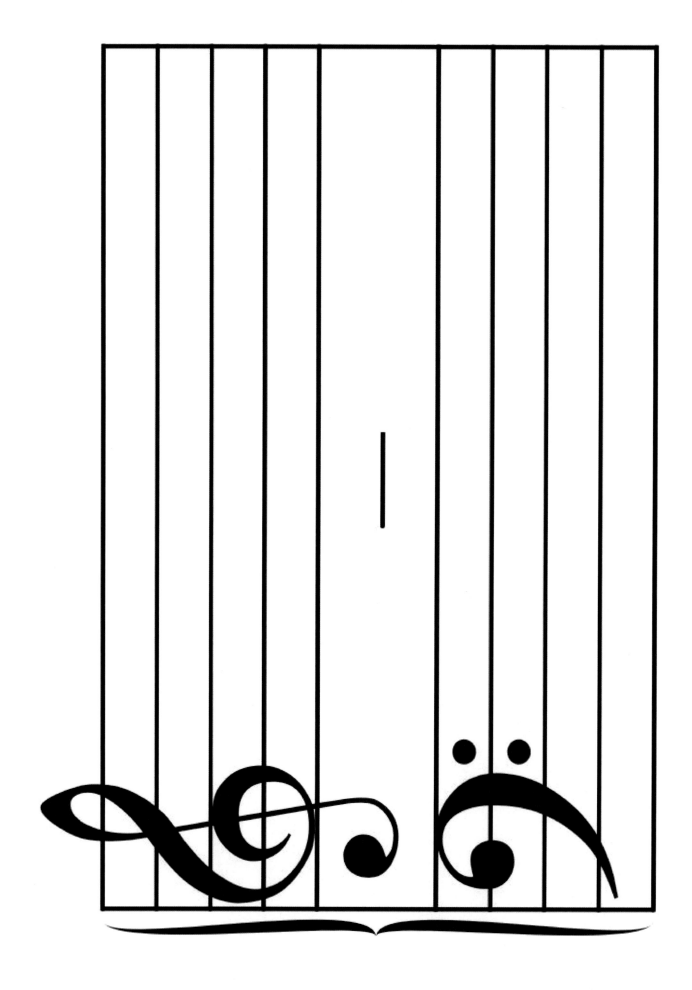

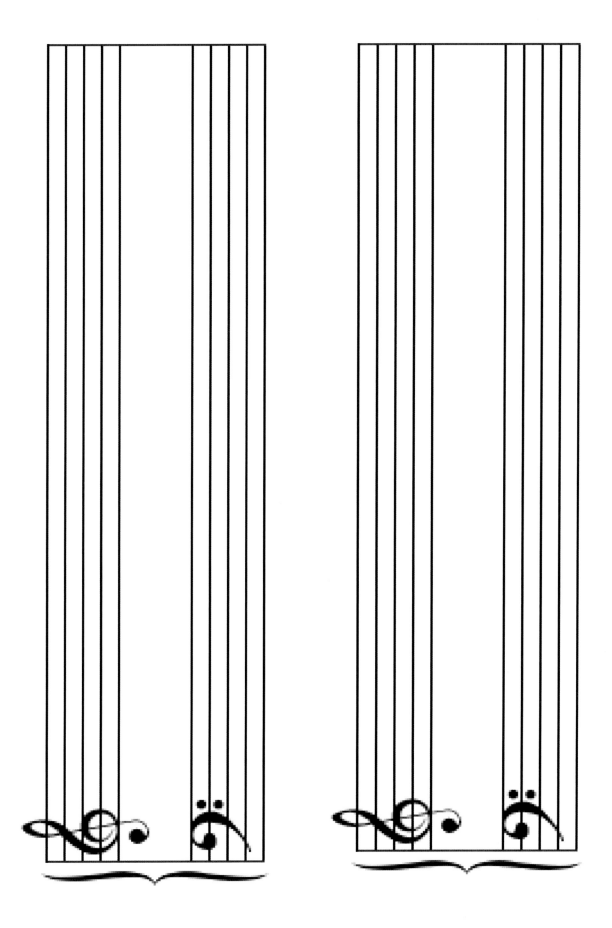

ABOUT THE AUTHORS

Karen & Michelle . . .
Mothers, sisters, teachers, women who are passionate
about educating kids.
We are dedicated to lifelong learning.

Karen, a mother of four, who has homeschooled her kids for more than eight years with her husband, Bob, has a bachelor's degree in child development with an emphasis in education. She lives in Utah where she gardens, teaches piano, and plays an excruciating number of board games with her kids. Karen is our resident Arts expert and English guru {most necessary as Michelle regularly and carelessly mangles the English language and occasionally steps over the bounds of polite society}.

Michelle and her husband, Cameron, homeschooling now for over a decade, teach their six boys on their ten acres in beautiful Idaho country. Michelle earned a bachelors in biology, making her the resident Science expert, though she is mocked by her friends for being the *Botanist with the Black Thumb of Death*. She also is the go-to for History and Government. She believes in staying up late, hot chocolate, and a no whining policy. We both pitch in on Geography, in case you were wondering, and are on a continual quest for knowledge.

*Visit our constantly updated blog for tons of free ideas,
free printables, and more cool stuff for sale:
www.Layers-of-Learning.com*

Made in the USA
Middletown, DE
07 January 2022

58118978R00024